Forew

Carp Fishing Knots
From the reel to the hook

This publication should help you
to gain a solid base of reliable,
tried and tested knots, enabling
you to land more fish.

Thanks to all the people, angling
professionals, fishing magazines and
tackle manufacturers for their advice,
support and encouragement in
helping create this unique publication.

Protect the environment and
save money by losing less tackle.

Tight lines and Strong knots.

Copyright Notice

No part of this document may be
reproduced in any form or by
any means without permission
in writing from:

Andy Steer

info@anglingknots.com

Legend

 Moisten   *Super glue*

 Trim   *Lighter*

Contents

Carp knots set-up   04
Spool knot   05
Double grinner knot   06
Improved Albright knot   07
Mahin leader knot   08
Leadcore splice   09
Needle knot   10
Grinner knot   11
Palomar knot   12
Jim Gibbinson knot   13
Mahseer knot   14
Braid ring knot   15
Figure of eight loop   16
Surgeon's loop   17
Domhof knot   18
Knotless knot   19
Hair loop   20
Half blood knot   21
Kryston non-slip loop   22
D-rig knot   23
Chod loop   24
Combi-link knot   25
Multi-hair rig   26
Whipped hair   27
Banded knotless knot   28
Bait floss knot   29
Distance marker/stop knot   30

Carp Fishing Knots Set-up

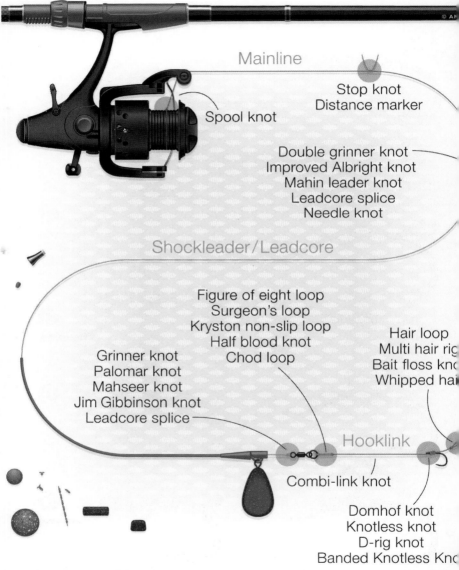

Mainline

Stop knot
Distance marker

Spool knot

Double grinner knot
Improved Albright knot
Mahin leader knot
Leadcore splice
Needle knot

Shockleader / Leadcore

Figure of eight loop
Surgeon's loop
Kryston non-slip loop
Half blood knot
Chod loop

Hair loop
Multi hair rig
Bait floss kno
Whipped hai

Grinner knot
Palomar knot
Mahseer knot
Jim Gibbinson knot
Leadcore splice

Hooklink

Combi-link knot

Domhof knot
Knotless knot
D-rig knot
Banded Knotless Kno

The carp fishing knots set-up shows the basic carp fishing
line connections and knots.

Spool Knot

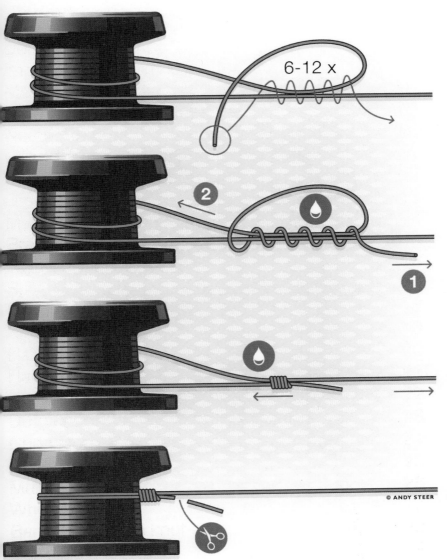

6-12 x

© ANDY STEER

The spool knot is used to attach the mainline to the spool. For extra line grip, wrap a piece of insulation tape around the spool and over the knot.

Double Grinner Knot

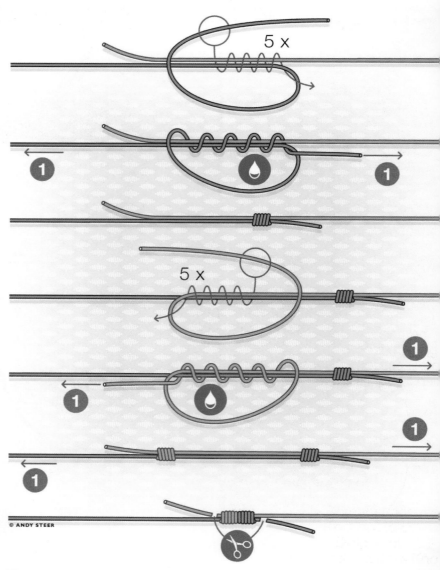

The double grinner/uni-uni knot is a good choice for joining mono to mono or mono to braid. Make five turns with mono, five to ten turns with braid.

Improved Albright Knot

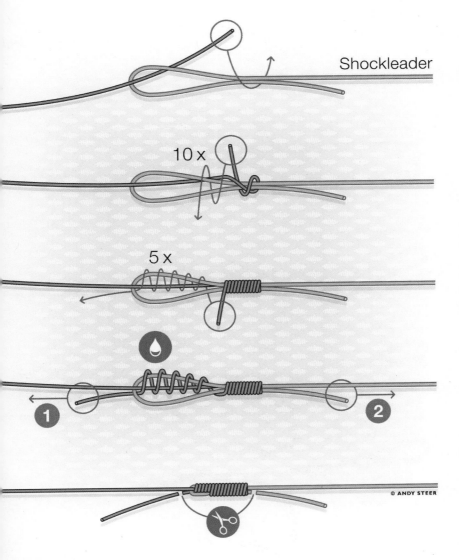

Shockleader

10 x

5 x

1 2

© ANDY STEER

The improved Albright knot is a good strong connection for attaching your shock leader to the main line. A low profile knot that will readily pass through your rod rings.

07

Mahin Leader Knot

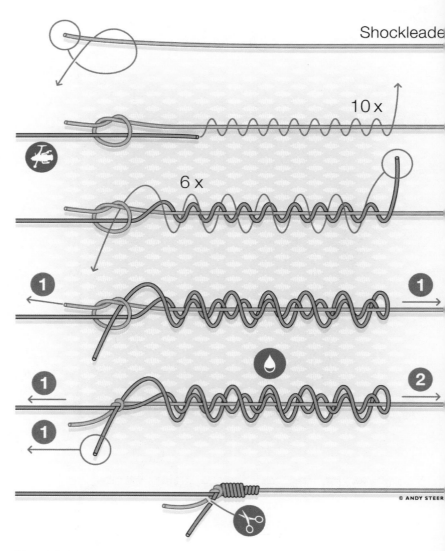

Shockleade

10 x

6 x

© ANDY STEER

The Mahin leader knot is a very strong tapered connection for attaching your shock leader to the main line. A low profile knot that will readily pass through your rod rings.

Leadcore Splice

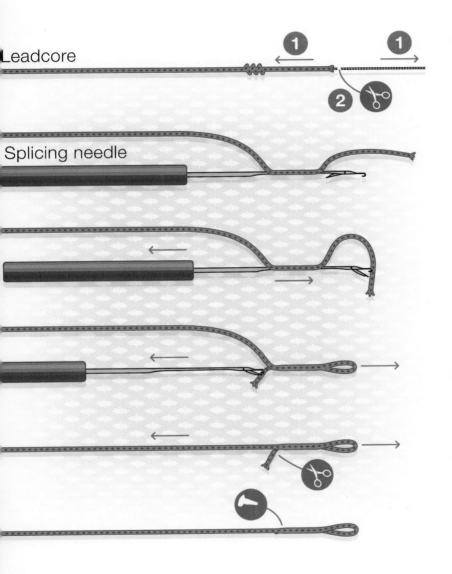

Leadcore

1 **1**

2

Splicing needle

The leadcore splice works on the chinese finger trap
principle, as the outside braid is pulled tight it constricts
and pulls tight on the inner braid.

Needle Knot

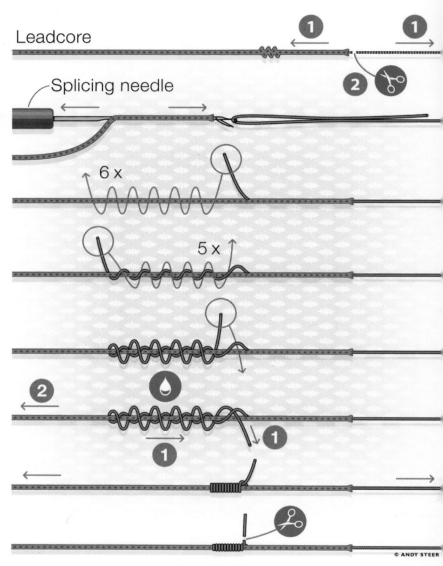

Leadcore

Splicing needle

6 x
5 x

Use the needle knot to attach your mainline to a lead core leader. The small diameter of the needle knot allows swivels and beads to easily pass over the knot.

Grinner Knot

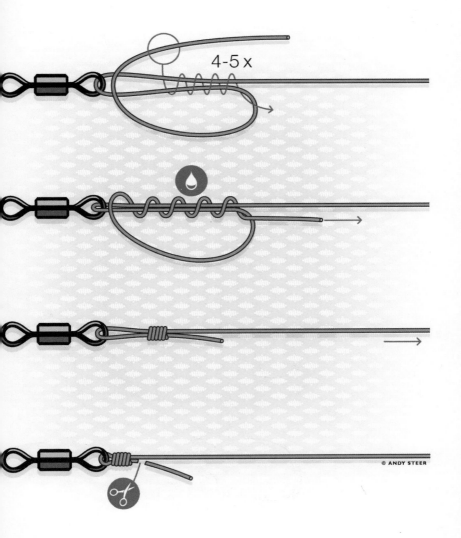

The grinner knot/uni-knot is a strong and reliable knot for attaching hooks and swivels.

Palomar Knot

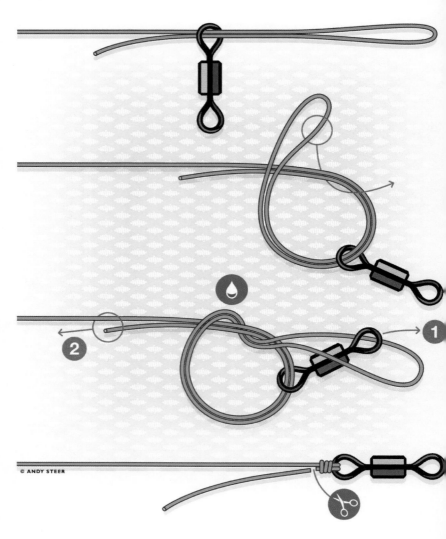

© ANDY STEER

The palomar knot is a reliable and easy to tie knot for attaching swivels and hooks.

Jim Gibbinson Knot

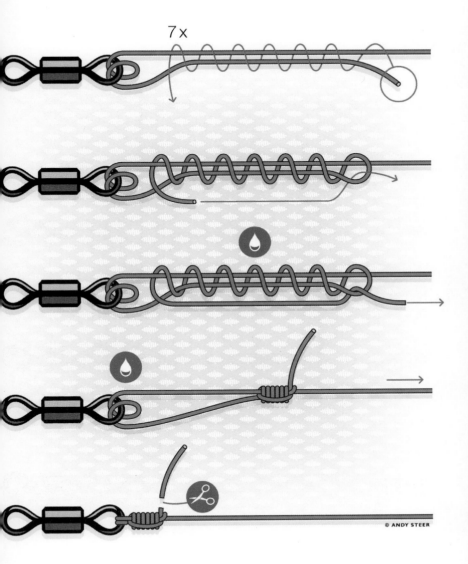

© ANDY STEER

The Jim Gibbinson knot is a robust, strong and reliable knot. Ideal for attaching a swivel to the mainline.

Mahseer Knot

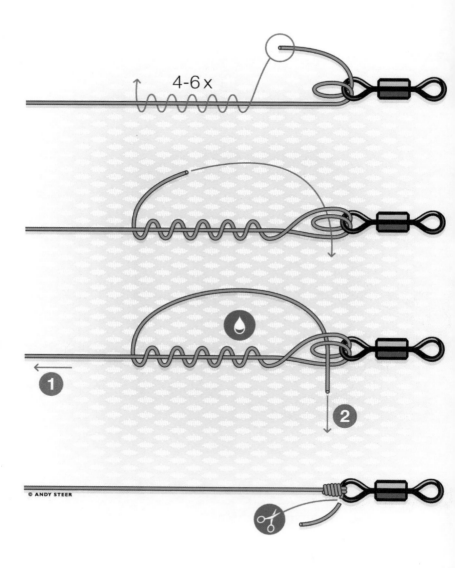

4-6 x

The mahseer knot/Trilene knot is a good choice for tying monofilament and fluorocarbon line to hooks and swivels. 15 lb line 4 x, 12 lb line 5 x, 10 lb line 6 x.

Braid Ring Knot

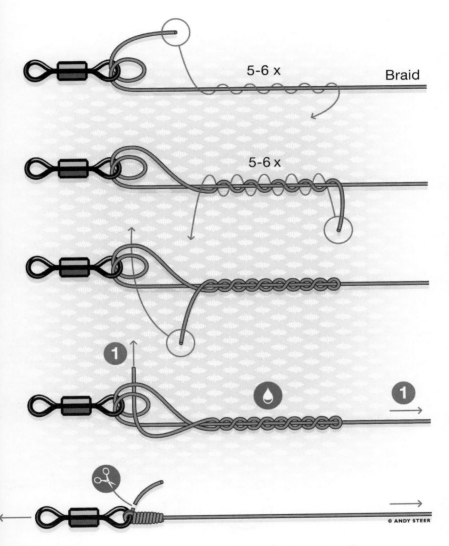

The braid ring knot is good solid knot for connecting braided line to swivels and terminal tackle.

Figure Of Eight Loop

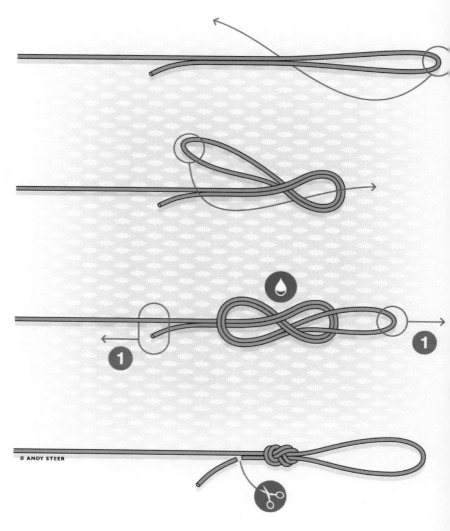

The figure of eight loop knot is an extremely strong loop knot for attaching swivels and clips.

Surgeon's Loop

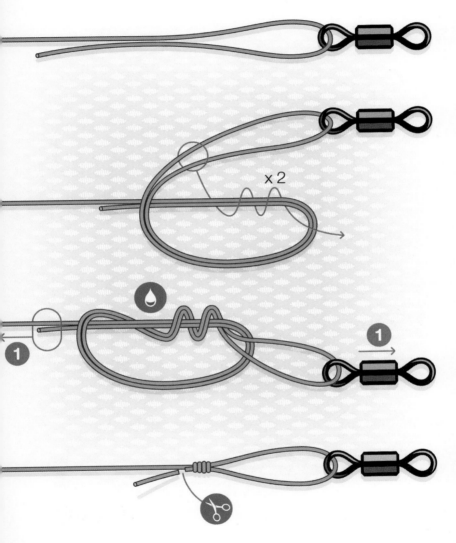

The surgeon's loop or double overhand loop knot is a quick and reliable way to form a loop.

Domhof Knot

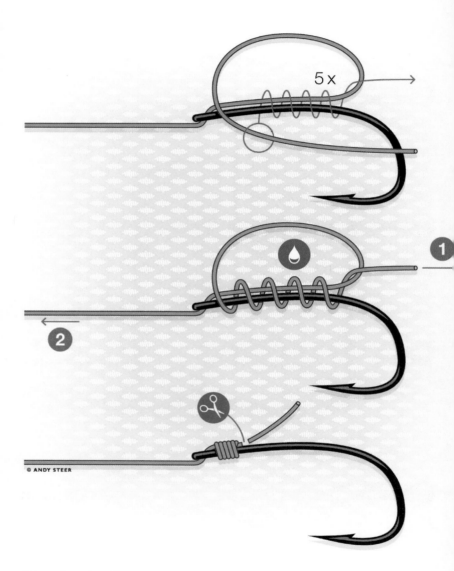

The domhof knot is a strong and neat knot for attaching the hook, often used in tying the chod rig and the hinged stiff rig.

Knotless Knot

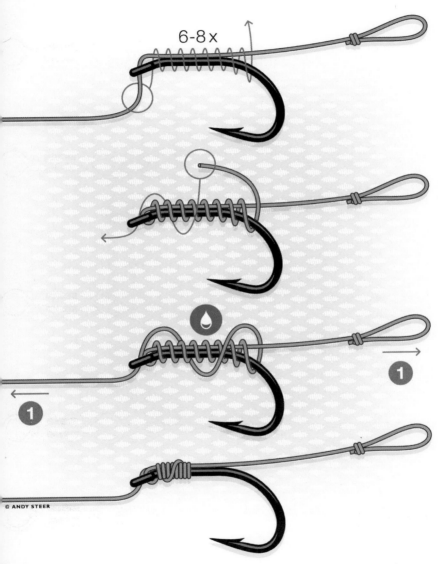

The knotless knot is the easiest and reliable way to make a hair rig.

Hair Loop

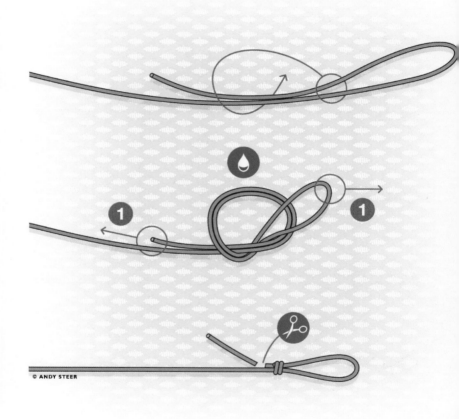

© ANDY STEER

The hair loop is a simple overhand loop knot.
This loop is for your boilie stop to secure the boilie/pellet in place.

Half Blood Knot

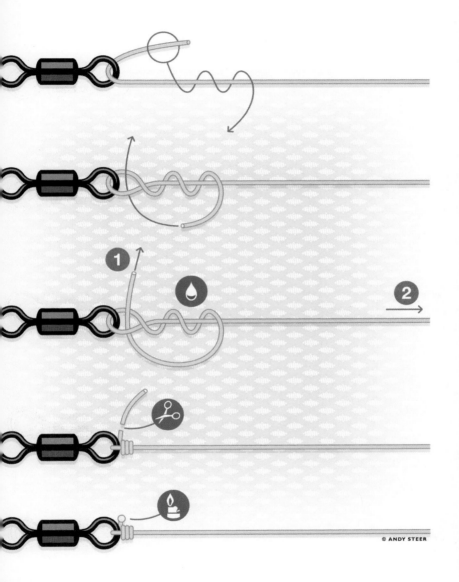

The half blood knot is a good way to attach swivels to thick mono/fluorocarbon line.

Kryston Non-Slip Loop

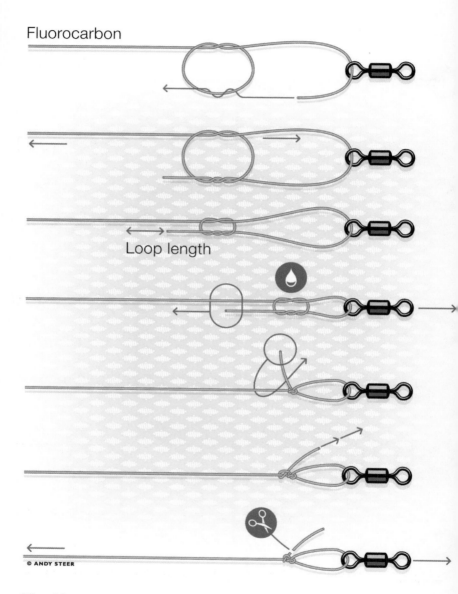

Fluorocarbon

Loop length

© ANDY STEER

The Kryston non-slip loop, a strong loop knot that allows the hooklink to move freely.

D Rig Knot

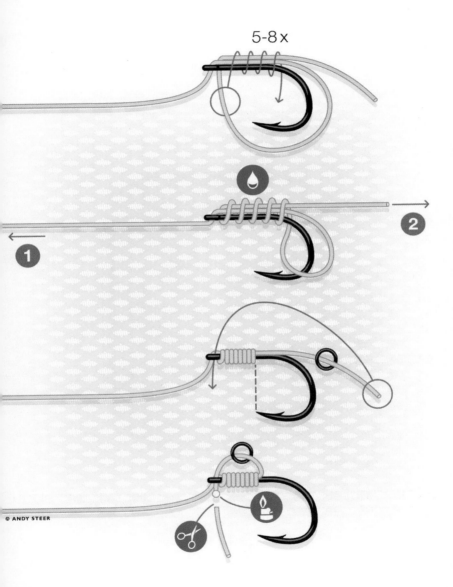

The D rig knot, probably the best knot for tying chods and hinged stiff links. Much neater than the knotless knot.

Chod Loop

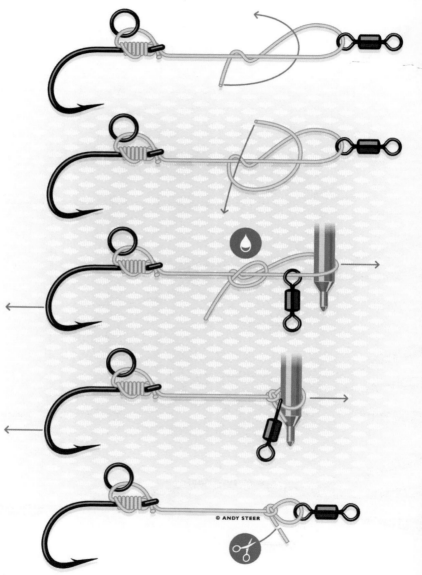

The chod loop, a strong loop knot that allows the hooklink to move freely.

Combi-Link Knot

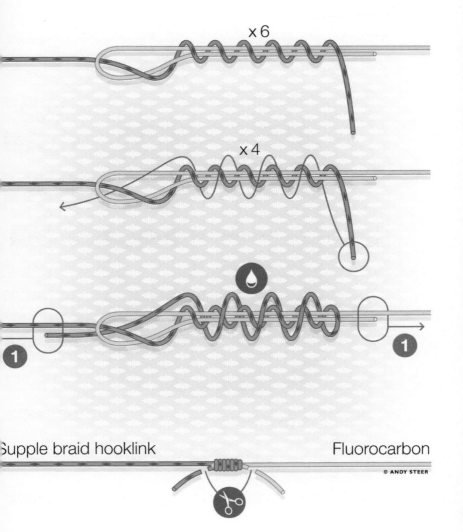

Supple braid hooklink   Fluorocarbon

© ANDY STEER

The combi-link knot is a neat and secure way to connect a supple braid to stiff fluorocarbon.

Multi-Hair Rig

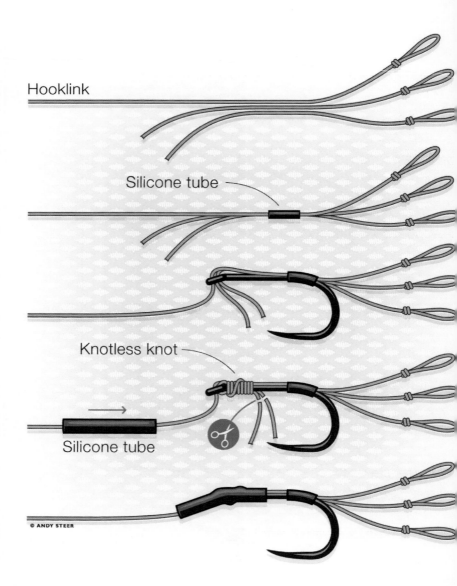

Hooklink

Silicone tube

Knotless knot

Silicone tube

© ANDY STEER

The multi-hair rig can be very productive when presenting smaller baits.

Whipped hair

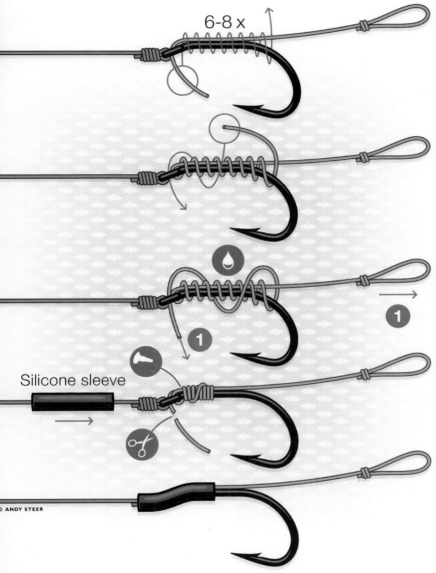

Silicone sleeve

Use the whipped hair knot to simply add a hair loop to the hook.

Banded Knotless Knot

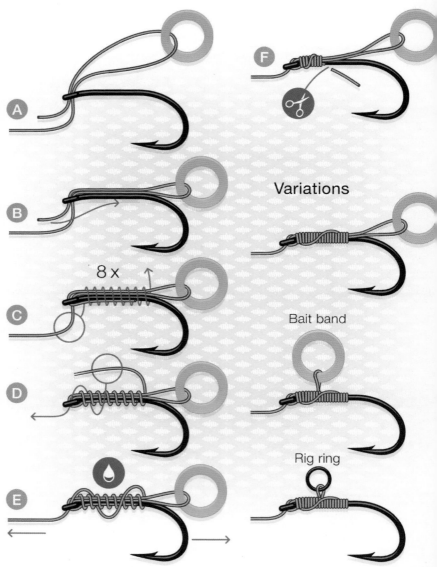

Variations

Bait band

Rig ring

Use the banded knotless knot to add a bait band or rig ring to the hook.

Bait Floss Knot

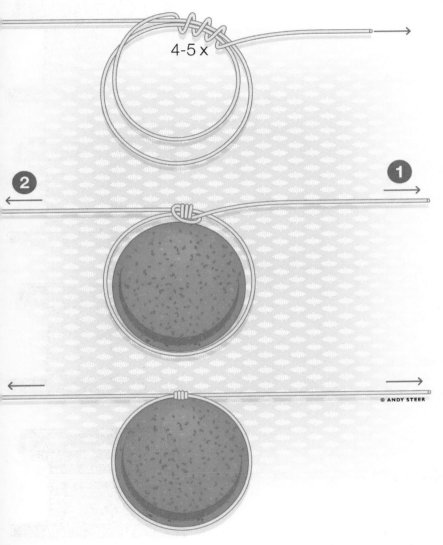

4-5 x

© ANDY STEER

Use the bait floss knot to attach a pop-up boilie to your rig ring, finish off with a double overhand knot and blob the floss ends with a lighter.

Distance Marker / Stop Knot

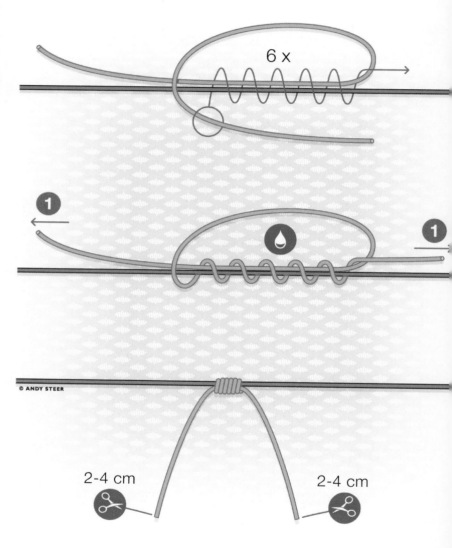

The distance marker/stop knot is the ideal knot for marking the fishing distance on your line or preventing your float from slipping.

Printed in Great Britain
by Amazon